BRITAIN IN OLD PHOTOGRAPHS

THE BARNETS
& HADLEY

BARNET & DISTRICT
LOCAL HISTORY SOCIETY

SUTTON PUBLISHING LIMITED

Sutton Publishing Limited
Phoenix Mill · Thrupp · Stroud
Gloucestershire · GL5 2BU

First published 1996

British Library Cataloguing in Publication Data
A catalogue record for this book is available from the
British Library.

ISBN 0-7509-1109-3

Typeset in 10/12 Perpetua.
Typesetting and origination by
Sutton Publishing Limited.
Printed in Great Britain by
Ebenezer Baylis, Worcester.

CONTENTS

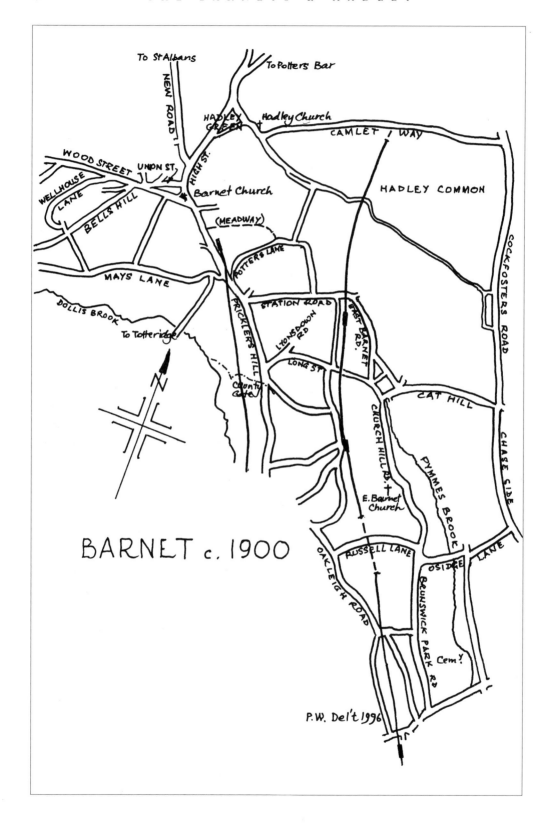

BARNET c. 1900

P.W. Del't 1996

Above is a view from the church tower looking south, *c.* 1930. The road is particularly wide below the church because this is where the market and fair used to be held (*see* page 31). This section of the lower end of the High Street is still recognizable today despite the changes in use of the buildings. The Bull Arts Centre occupies the old public house and Clark's the drapers is in the process of becoming a restaurant. The future of the National Westminster Bank building on the corner of Park Road is currently in doubt. It was built in 1892 as the London County and Westminster Bank Ltd.

An aerial view of Barnet, *c.* 1910. It shows the church and the houses in Wood Street, including Church House and the rear of the council offices. The High Street can be seen running northwards, with St Alban's Road leading off to the north-west.

The changeover from trams to trolley buses took place in Barnet in 1937, but both systems terminated at the same point, just south of the church of St John the Baptist. The changeover involved moving the war memorial forward on to a roundabout. The upper photograph, taken in about 1920, shows a queue of people waiting to board a tram. Behind them can be seen the shop belonging to John A. Clark & Son, who sold all sorts of haberdashery. The shop was founded in 1887 at 66 High Street and survived until 1979. The lower picture shows a trolley bus parked outside Salmon & Son at 70 High Street.

Barnet High Street, *c*. 1910. This view includes a wide range of means of transport, including a bicycle, a car, a tram and a horse-drawn carriage. It even has a rather comfortable-looking pram on the pavement in front of the churchyard railings.

This is the same stretch of the High Street but this time looking northwards. The war memorial had been installed to the south of the church in about 1922.

The public house seen on the left in both these views of the High Street is currently known as the Dandy Lion although we understand its name is to change once more. First referred to in 1439, it was then known as the Antelope, having previously been called the Cardinal's Hat. It had been rebuilt as the Red Lion by 1720 and extended southwards across what is now Fitzjohn Avenue. It was rebuilt in 1890 and again in about 1930. In 1792 the Barnet Association met at the Red Lion Inn to confirm the continuation of an association formed to prosecute burglars, robbers and others who committed offences in Barnet and the neighbouring parishes. Rewards were offered to inhabitants of the various parishes who enabled the prosecution of an offender to take place. The money for the rewards was to come from the members of the association.

The upper section of the High Street, looking southwards back towards the church, *c*. 1900. The building in the photograph with the arched windows is the old post office, which in 1913 became the site of the Barnet Palace cinema and later that of the Waitrose supermarket until this latter shop moved into the newly built Spires complex. Eric Daw in his *Barnet High Street in the Early 20th Century* recalled his visits to the Palace:

'Whenever an attractive programme was advertised, I would beg my mother to let me go to the Saturday matinee, the seats for children costing 2½*d*, 5*d*., 9*d*. and 1/3*d*. If I went alone, or with a school friend, 5*d*., plus a penny or two for a sherbert dab or an ice-cream, was the sum usually given to me; if, however, I went with an older sister, the luxury of a 9*d*. or even a 1/3*d*. seat at the back would come my way. On one occasion I bought a 2½*d*. ticket for a seat in the front two rows, with the idea of spending the remaining 2½*d*. of my 5*d*. on riotous living at the nearest sweet shop. Being obliged to look up at enormous, fuzzy and distorted images on the screen, in the midst of noisy boys bobbing up and down on their seats with excitement, gave me nothing but eyestrain, a stiff neck, and a flea; so thereafter I kept my company with the rather more sedate 5*d*. patrons.'

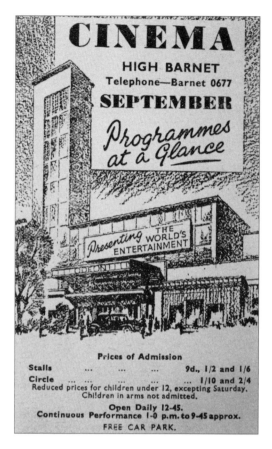

There were two cinemas in Barnet. The Odeon, which is still open, lies at the bottom of Barnet Hill and was built in 1935. The Barnet Cinema, which was also called the Cinema Palace and, from 1955, the Gaumont, opened on 26 December 1912 and ran until August 1959. The building was demolished in 1961. A fire damaged the cinema in 1934 and its tall arched front was replaced with one of a plainer, contemporary style, with a café and dance hall added over the entrance hall.

The High Street looking south towards the church. This photograph must have been taken before 1875 since the Hertfordshire spike on top of the church tower can be seen in the background. The lower view is a later one taken in about 1912. The proposed Barnet shopping centre had been debated for over fifty years. Finally, in 1986, plans were agreed by the London Borough of Barnet to develop the area behind the Methodist Church as a shopping precinct, leaving the spires of the church to form the entrance and provide a name.

Queen Elizabeth's Boys' School. In 1573 Queen Elizabeth granted a charter to the Town of Barnet for a 'Common Grammar School' '. . . for the education, bringing up, and instruction of boys and youths, to be brought up in grammar and other learning'. In 1873 the Visitors of the Jesus Hospital charity were authorised to contribute £5,000 to build new classrooms and a yearly sum of £400 towards the maintenance of the school. The upper photograph shows the Tudor Hall and the headmaster's house from Wood Street while the lower picture shows the new classrooms that were built in 1873.

This sketch was drawn in 1923 by Frank Collier who was the Art Master at Queen Elizabeth's Boys' School. The classrooms can be seen behind the mulberry tree and on the right is the Tudor Hall, in which the school first opened.

The 1873 classrooms have been extended, the mulberry tree is seen without its leaves and the rear of the Tudor Hall and the headmaster's house are on the right. The Endowed Schools Act of 1869 meant that since Queen Elizabeth's was an endowed school it had to submit re-organisation plans. These plans received the royal sanction in 1873 and in view of the forthcoming changes the Governors decided to close the school at Easter 1873 as a temporary measure.

The Barnet Museum – taken before the building was closed for restoration in 1979, when the museum collection was held in 31 & 33 Wood Street.

Following a meeting held on 14 March 1927 the Barnet Record Society was formed with the aim of collecting historical 'records' relating to the area. In 1938, after storage of the material elsewhere, the collection finally found a permanent home at 31 Wood Street, with the use of the ground floor of no. 33. The Second World War interrupted work at the museum but it re-opened in 1946. Following the discovery of dry rot in 1979 the museum had to close once again but it re-opened in March 1983 in the refurbished 31 Wood Street; no. 33 was sold for commercial redevelopment to offset some of the cost.

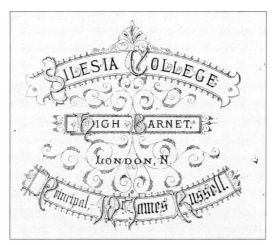

Silesia College. According to Cecil Tripp, when Queen Elizabeth's Grammar School was temporarily closed at Easter 1873, the master, Charles Presdee, opened a preparatory school at Silesia House, Bells Hill, Barnet (*see* page 17). Silesia College dates its establishment as a boys' boarding school to 1878. It later became known as Hertford County College, New Barnet, when in 1895 it moved to Whittinghame Lodge in Station Road. Mr Herbert Catford had bought the Barnet school in about 1890 and he purchased Whittinghame Lodge in 1894. It was subsequently called Norfolk Court. The new fire station now occupies the site.

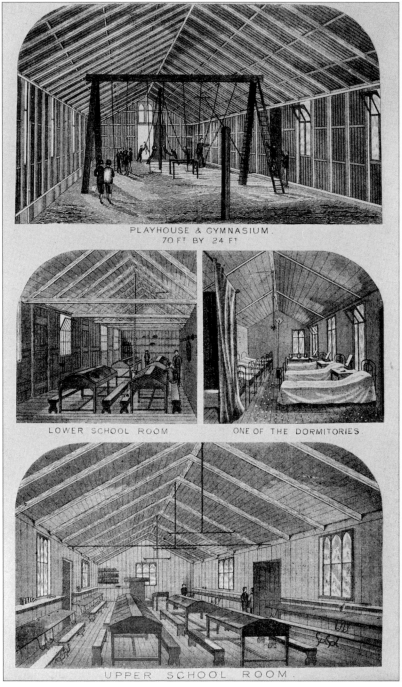

PLAYHOUSE & GYMNASIUM.
70 FT BY 24 FT

LOWER SCHOOL ROOM   ONE OF THE DORMITORIES

UPPER SCHOOL ROOM.

Interior of Silesia College, Bells Hill, c. 1880. In 1894 the fees varied from 24 to 45 guineas per annum. The headmaster was Mr Raleigh M. Gilbert and the matron Miss F. Edwards. An advertisement for the school claimed that the headmaster 'has been continuously engaged since 1869 in Middle and Upper Middle Class Education', that the 'Playing Field, Playground, Gymnasium, and Tepid Swimming Bath, afford every facility for Physical Recreation' and that the 'Schoolrooms are large and well fitted with modern furniture and apparatus'.

Christ Church in St Albans Road was built on land bought in 1844 by Captain Trotter of Dyrham Park from George Byng. In 1855 a north aisle was added to the church and a gallery was installed at the west end of the new part for orphans of the Crimean War. One of the most famous members of the congregation was David Livingstone, who attended the church whilst he lived on Hadley Green in 1857/8. (*See* page 126.)

Christ Church vicarage, also built by Captain Trotter. A National School was built adjoining the church, where services were held until the church itself was completed in 1845/6. These school buildings are now used by the Red Cross.

This elaborate design was produced for the front cover of a programme for an old boys' reunion for Christ Church Boys' School, Alston Road, held in 1901. This was the first of the old boys' dinners organized by Mr John Brown, the school's headmaster for forty-two years. The cost of the entire dinner was £20 8s 4d and it was attended by a hundred past pupils.

This is the back cover of the 1901 programme, showing a picture of the school building and the church. The Cambridge don and local historian Dr Frederick Brittain, in his autobiography, describes these reunions as 'a Society for the Veneration of "Gaffer", as he [Mr Brown] was affectionately called'. The Boys' school opened in 1879/80 at a cost of £1,001. Until 1932 it was an all-age school for boys and eventually became a mixed school in the 1960s. In 1968 the school moved to Byng Road.

The Revd William Pennefather, who came to Christ Church in 1852, photographed in the vicarage garden. (*See* page 125.)

The Iron Room, where conferences were held, was erected by the Revd William Pennefather in the field to the north of Christ Church. Mr Sydney Bevan is standing by the lamp-post.

A group of boys photographed in Alston Road. Could they have been from Christ Church school? Alston Road was built in about 1875.

A fire in the High Street, *c.* 1908. The Exchange Buildings, which had been built in 1891 on the corner of the St Albans Road, can be seen in the distance.

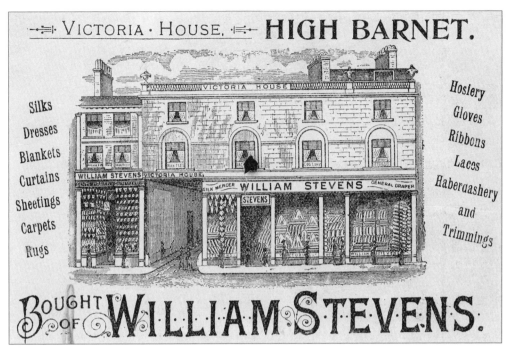

William Stevens began his outfitters business in 1886 and his brother Charles opened a grocers further along the High Street on the corner of Moxon Street. In 1898 Kelly's Directory showed William Stevens occupying both 72 and 74 High Street. When the shop closed in 1964 it was being run by William's grandson, Charles B. Stevens. The Red Lion Inn, in which in 1667 Pepys consumed the best cheese cakes he had ever had, occupied 72, 74 and 76 High Street.

Mitchell's Furnishing Stores in Union Street. The 1925 Kelly's Directory shows John Mitchell occupying the Barnet Auction Rooms at no. 1a, but in 1926 Harry John Nickolds is at that address. Between 1892 and 1914 the Young Women's Christian Association occupied no. 1.

Victoria Cottage Hospital. Opened in 1888 to commemorate Queen Victoria's Golden Jubilee, the hospital was extended ten years later to commemorate her Diamond Jubilee. In 1924 the hospital moved to Wood Street and later became the Victoria Maternity Hospital which was refurbished and developed in 1995 and converted into flats.

Queen Elizabeth's Girls' school was opened in 1888, in premises adjacent to the Cottage Hospital. The school was extended and a new hall and classrooms were opened by HRH the Duchess of Kent on 4 November 1938.

Wellhouse Hospital, 1918. The 1834 Poor Law Reform Act provided for the formation of Unions, which were formed from several parishes joining together to provide services under the Act and appointing officers known as guardians. The Barnet Guardians bought just over three acres of land, previously part of the common, in Wellhouse Lane at a cost of £182. The same year they built the workhouse to house people from the surrounding parishes which were part of the Union. The workhouse closed in 1939 but some of the old workhouse buildings remain and now form a small part of the complex of hospital buildings. During the First World War the main block of the present hospital was built to accommodate casualties. It had six 26-bed wards. After the war the military hospital was handed over to the Guardians. In 1948 the Wellhouse became a National Health hospital and in 1951 it became Barnet General Hospital.

Wellhouse Farm and the physic well stood on land which was formerly part of Barnet Common. William Camden, in his book *Britannica*, published in 1586, refers to a medicinal spring at Barnet. The therapeutic qualities of the spring water were renowned in the seventeenth century. Samuel Pepys wrote that on 11 July 1664 he swallowed five glasses of water and afterwards visited the Red Lion Inn (near the church) where he enjoyed the cheese cakes. The well lies off Wellhouse Lane and is now housed in a mock Tudor building, shown in the lower print, which was erected in 1937.

The Fair at Barnet in 1845. The name Chipping is derived from the Anglo-Saxon word 'ceap' meaning bargain, and indicates that Barnet held a market in ancient times. On 23 August 1199 King John granted a Charter to the Abbot and monks of St Albans, allowing a market 'in the vill of Barnet on one day in the week, to wit, Thursday . . .'. On 6 February 1588 Queen Elizabeth I granted a Charter to the Lord of the Manor of Barnet giving the right to hold a weekly market on Mondays, and a twice-yearly fair. The Cockney rhyming slang for hair is Barnet – which is short for Barnet Fair.

Barnet Fair was held on land at the bottom of Barnet Hill in the early part of this century. St Catherine's Roman Catholic primary school and the Vale Drive Clinic now stand on the site.

The site of the fairground. This is a similar view to the previous one but taken from further back. The row of cottages was known as the Potteries. Could there be a link between these buildings and the ancient Potters Lane which lies on the opposite side of the Great North Road, just below the railway bridge? A block of flats on the site now carries the name.

This row of fifteen cottages was acquired in 1804 by the parishes of St Andrew Holborn above Bar and St George the Martyr for their 'infant poor'. The cottages were later used to provide accommodation for the orphans of soldiers killed in the Crimean war. The building in the background was used as a lodging house.

This farm is variously referred to as Underhill Farm and Sharp's Farm. According to the Kelly's Directory of 1929 Thomas Sharp was then living at Underhill Farm.

The Old Red Lion, 1940s. On the left, behind the older pub, is the gable of the 1930s-built Old Red Lion, which replaced the original nineteenth-century pub. The older building was known as Underhill Lodge until its demolition in 1954.

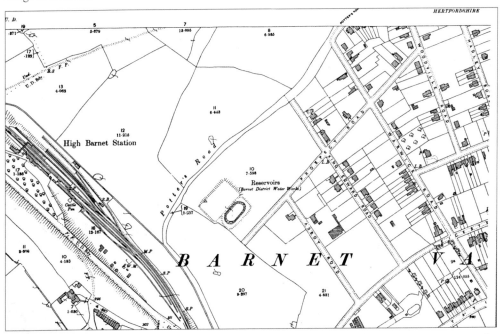

This section of the 1896 Ordnance Survey map shows the group of buildings featured on pages 32–4. The route of this section of road up Barnet Hill was straightened in 1818 by the Whetstone Turnpike Trust and in 1823 they altered the gradient by forming an embankment. The surveyor who undertook the work was Sir James McAdam. Previously the road had passed directly in front of the cottages and climbed the hill to emerge at Victoria Lane.

Views of Barnet station taken in about 1890. The branch line to High Barnet was opened in 1872 and was built by the Great Northern Railway Company. The station was sited at the bottom of Barnet Hill rather than on the other suggested sites of Wood Street or Hadley Green. In 1940 the line was electrified and went through the newly constructed tunnel at East Finchley to join up with the tube line.

A tram going under the railway bridge over the Great North Road at Underhill. Trams finally ceased in London in 1952.

On 7 August 1953 a train over-ran the shunting neck and crashed down the embankment alongside the bridge at this spot. The lead coach had to be supported with sleepers to stop it rolling on to the Great North Road.

A view of the bottom of Barnet Hill, taken in about 1890, shows the Queens Arms. The earliest reference to this pub was in 1862 when the owner and licensee was a Charles James Chaloner. In 1928 the pub closed down on this site and was rebuilt on the other side of the road.

Newton & Son were 'motor engineers' according to the 1929 Kelly's Directory. The garage was demolished in 1972 shortly after this photograph was taken. A complex of flats has now been built on this corner.

The road now known as the Meadway was a footpath which linked Barnet with East Barnet Valley, until it was developed in 1930.

NEW BARNET

*The steep banks of the Great Northern Railway line run across the centre of this aerial view, taken in about
1910. In 1850 the railway cut through an estate known as Lyonsdown to the south east of Barnet, where
Barnet station was opened. The railway opened in August 1850. Eliza Cook's Journal of October 1851
describes a journey from King's Cross station on the newly built line: 'In the fields alongside the
embankment on which we run, the lazy cows are whisking their sides, udder-deep amidst the green grass;
they are passed in an instant. But look beyond. Along the rising ground on the hill-top is scattered an old
English town, with many snug dwellings of the opulent and comfortable lying about it. "That is Barnet," says
a fellow traveller.'*

This water fountain was originally put up on the Triangle at the centre of New Barnet. However, it was later moved to the nearby Victoria Park, where it still stands. On one side of the fountain are the words 'Honest water which ne'er left man in the mire. The gift of T. Morgan Harvey.' On the other side it reads 'Metropolitan Drinking Fountain and Cattle Trough Association'. A drinking trough for horses and cattle was sited alongside the Triangle in the road.

The Triangle in the early 1920s. The war memorial was erected in about 1922 and the original brick arched railway bridge can be seen spanning East Barnet Road.

Station Road. Barclays Bank until recently occupied the left-hand side of the building shown in the centre, while the estate agents Ferguson Taylor had offices on the right-hand side. On 12 September 1886 a number of local residents, headed by Edward Ferguson Taylor, wrote to Messrs Sharples, Teeke, Lucas and Seebohn at Hitchin asking that they open a branch of their bank in New Barnet. This letter was displayed in a wooden frame in the bank at 36 Station Road until it closed in 1995.

The East Barnet Town Hall. This building was designed by Frederick Shenton and opened in June 1892. The East Barnet Valley Board had been set up in 1873 and was superseded in 1894 by the East Barnet Valley Urban District Council. In 1988 the London Borough of Barnet, having no further use for the building, decided to sell it and after standing empty for a number of years it has this year (1996) become a restaurant.

Lytton Road. The names of many of the roads in New Barnet are connected with Sir E. Bulwer Lytton, whose book *The Last of the Barons* describes the Battle of Barnet. The parade of shops featured in the centre survives today but the buildings on both sides of Station Road have been redeveloped. On the left stood Grafenburg House, which was used as a hydropathic establishment by Richard Metcalfe in 1876.

Station Road, looking towards the railway bridge, *c.* 1900. This was the first road to be built in the area that was to become New Barnet. It linked the Great North Road with the new 'Barnet' station and was initially called New Road.

Station Road, looking away from the railway bridge, a few years later than the previous photograph. The spire of the Congregational Church, which stood on the corner of Plantagenet Road and Station Road, can be seen behind the houses. Along Station Road large, prestigious houses were built to provide homes for middle-class commuters travelling by train into the city to work. Those on the left-hand side are currently used as offices but those on the right, with the large porches and rooms above, are still in residential use.

The demolition of the Wesleyan Methodist Church on the corner of Lyonsdown Road and Station Road, 1963. A steeplejack suffered a fatal fall during the demolition process. Kingmaker House, an office block, now stands on the site.

The Congregational Church with, inset, its minister, the Revd J. Alford Davies. In October 1900 he had judged the elocution competetion at the local Eisteddfod held at the Assembly Rooms, Lytton Road. The Eisteddfod was run by the New Barnet Literary and Debating Society, which had been founded in 1874 as the New Barnet Young Men's Mutual Improvement Society. The ministers of the local churches were very involved in the establishment of the society. The first public meeting took place in the Baptist Chapel. The Presbyterian minister, the Revd George Drysdale, opened the meeting, and a lecture was given by the Revd J. Mountain of St James's Church. The meeting was closed by the Congregational minister, the Revd George Twentyman. The Baptist, Congregational and Presbyterian ministers were all vice-presidents of the society.

St Augustine's Presbyterian Church stood on the corner of Somerset Road and Plantagenet Road. Founded in 1870, it was replaced by St John's when the old Congregational Church and the Presbyterian Church merged in 1967 at a cost of £40,000. The architect was Jon Finlayson of Oakhurst Avenue, East Barnet, who won a civic award for his design.

Holy Trinity Church, Lyonsdown. Work on this church began in 1864 and was completed in 1865 but it was not consecrated until 1868. It was designed by Mr Ewan Christian, the architect for the London Diocese. The church stands on the corner of Somerset Road and Lyonsdown Road.

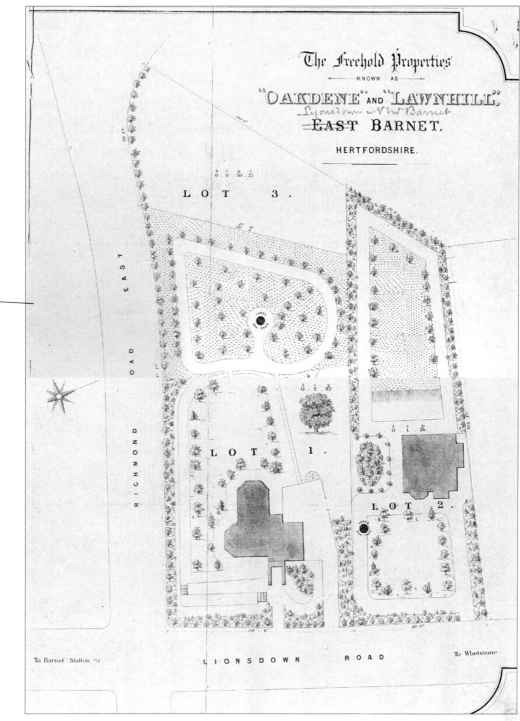

The Lyonsdown Estate was sold in 1849 to the Great Northern Railway Company to enable the construction of the railway to take place. The mansion was demolished in 1862 and the Lyonsdown estate was developed with some very grand houses. This plan shows two of them, built on the corner of Lyonsdown Road and Richmond Road.

This is 'Lot no. 1'. This house has survived and is now called SMA House; it is occupied by the Society of African Missions.

This is 'Lot no. 2', since demolished and replaced by flats.

Willenhall. In 1820 Thomas Wyatt built a mansion on the site of an earlier house called Belle Vue, so-named because it was sited on a raised piece of land. This area had at one time been the site of the manor mill, called Agate Mill, and is still referred to as County Gate. Wyatt called his house Willenhall House, after Willenhall in Warwickshire. By 1920 Willenhall Avenue had been laid out and the house had been demolished. The area was subsequently developed for housing.

H. PULLEN,

Butcher,

5, Station Rd., NEW BARNET

Telephone : Barnet 0188.

Prime English   Southdown
&   &
Scotch Beef.   Scotch Mutton.

Local shops to provide for the new community were soon established along both East Barnet Road and the section of Station Road that runs up towards the railway. Both H. Pullen at no. 5 and R.C. Spearman at 7 Station Road have disappeared and their premises have been replaced by office blocks. Mortgage Express now occupies 1 Lyonsdown Road, while the building that was used by British Telecom for a number of years is now being converted by the London Borough of Barnet into flats for short-term letting.

MAW'S MOTOR. FIRST WITH THE BEST GOODS!

George Maw, a Lincolnshire farmer, came to London in 1807. His company had started off in Aldersgate and a factory in Cromer Road, New Barnet, was opened in 1921. Five generations of the Maw family were subsequently involved in running the company, but it was sold to Vernons in 1980 and closed in 1982 when Vernons went into liquidation. Shortly afterwards the site was sold for redevelopment as housing. The lower photograph shows Maw's wages staff at work.

Rosa Morison House, Gloucester Road. The 1925 Kelly's Directory describes this as the Rosa Morison House of Recovery, with Sister Tattersall as the matron. It is currently used by the London Borough of Barnet as a day centre for people with severe physical and sensory disabilities.

Greenhill School, 78 Station Road. This was one of a number of small private schools in New Barnet. Nos 76 and 78 are currently occupied by the Thornbridge House Retirement Home.

The railway bridge over East Barnet Road. The Barnet Press in October 1936 reported the finding of a pre-Roman sword under the highway, during the 'recent excavation' in East Barnet Road. The railway divided New Barnet into two parts. On the whole the grander houses were on the side nearest High Barnet while the properties on the other side were smaller and the shops and small businesses more numerous.

East Barnet Road had a mixture of small shops. In 1980 a number of them were demolished when Sainsburys supermarket was opened on the site. The hall which stood halfway along on the right-hand side was used as a recording studio in the 1960s and was used by The Beatles, among others.

Gristwoods Furnishing Stores on the corner of East Barnet Road and Station Approach sold absolutely everything necessary to furnish a home, as this advertisement shows.

Further down East Barnet Road, beyond the junction with Margaret Road, houses took the place of shops. The public house on the right was known as the Cambridge Arms. This photograph was taken in about 1910.

The mangled remains after a fire which broke out on 9 January 1907 at Lockharts timber merchants premises in Lancaster Road, between the junctions with Margaret Road and Henry Road.

Margaret Road, near the junction with Lancaster Road. Work began on the Parochial Schools for boys, girls and infants in Margaret Road in August 1869. In 1882 the Commissioner of Police built the East Barnet police station on the corner of Margaret Road and Edward Road. In 1933 it was proposed to sell the station to cut costs and the building was used to provide short-term residential accommodation until it was demolished.

Henry Road. Samuel Walton snr had come to the New Barnet area in the 1860s and his family firm, Walton & Sons (Contractors & Builders), built some of the houses in St Wilfrid's Road and Henry Road. One son, Thomas Walton, and his family lived in Henry Road. He and his brother Samuel were both builders. Another brother, Zachariah, took over the Warwick Tavern in 1870 and appears to have owned Warwick Cottages, which he let.

The John Hampden Secondary School in Victoria Road was closed down following a fire in 1961/2 and the children were sent to a new school which was built on the site of Folly Farm. The site of the Victoria Road school has been developed by Ideal Homes Ltd as a housing estate called Mulberry Close. The old annex to the school is currently used by the New Barnet Residents Association as a community centre.

The Alexandra pub, at the junction of Victoria Road and East Barnet Road, was licensed as an alehouse in 1867. Chris and Nancy Tooley currently run the pub.

The Lasts' removal van. The Last family had several businesses. As well as removals, they also ran a market garden, initially in Bowes Road and later in Brookhill Road. This provided produce for their horse and cart trade and later for their greengrocers shops.

In 1961 Peter and Stanley Last took over the removal firm of Willis & Timpsons, which was based in East Barnet Road. The removal company still operates from the same premises.

The Frusher family ran the pork butchers shop on the corner of Victoria Road. They provided ham teas at their nearby Folly Farm, which had been leased in 1918 from Cosmo Bevan to Samuel Eli Frusher and Charles Bramwell Vassar Frusher.

Folly Farm stood on the edge of Hadley Woods. It is reputed to have some connection with Dick Turpin but this seems unlikely. There was, however, a Thomas Turpin living there in 1680.

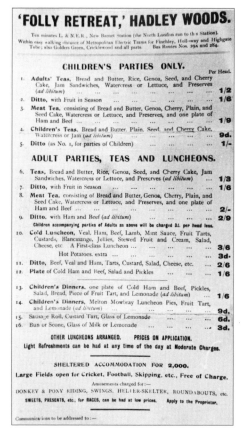

'FOLLY RETREAT,' HADLEY WOODS.

Ten minutes L. & N.E.R., New Barnet Station (the North London run to th s Station).
Within easy walking distance of Metropolitan Electric Trams for Finchley, Holloway and Highgate Tube; also Golders Green, Cricklewood and all parts. Bus Routes Nos. 29A and 284.

CHILDREN'S PARTIES ONLY.

		Per Head.
1.	Adults' Teas, Bread and Butter, Rice, Genoa, Seed, and Cherry Cake, Jam Sandwiches, Watercress or Lettuce, and Preserves (ad libitum)	1/2
2.	Ditto, with Fruit in Season	1/6
3.	Meat Tea, consisting of Bread and Butter, Genoa, Cherry, Plain, and Seed Cake, Watercress or Lettuce, and Preserves, and one plate of Ham and Beef	1/9
4.	Children's Teas, Bread and Butter, Plain, Seed, and Cherry Cake, Watercress or Jam (ad libitum)	9d.
5.	Ditto (as No. 1, for parties of Children)	1/-

ADULT PARTIES, TEAS AND LUNCHEONS.

6.	Teas, Bread and Butter, Rice, Genoa, Seed, and Cherry Cake, Jam Sandwiches, Watercress or Lettuce, and Preserves (ad libitum)	1/3
7.	Ditto, with Fruit in Season	1/6
8.	Meat Tea, consisting of Bread and Butter, Genoa, Cherry, Plain, and Seed Cake, Watercress or Lettuce, and Preserves, and one plate of Ham and Beef	2/-
9.	Ditto, with Ham and Beef (ad libitum)	2/9
	Children accompanying parties of Adults as above will be charged 3d. per head less.	
10.	Cold Luncheon, Veal, Ham, Beef, Lamb, Mint Sauce, Fruit Tarts, Custards, Blancmange, Jellies, Stewed Fruit and Cream, Salad, Cheese, etc. A First-class Luncheon	3/6
	Hot Potatoes, extra	3d.
11.	Ditto, Beef, Veal and Ham, Tarts, Custard, Salad, Cheese, etc.	2/6
12.	Plate of Cold Ham and Beef, Salad and Pickles	1/6
13.	Children's Dinners, one plate of Cold Ham and Beef, Pickles, Salad, Bread, Piece of Fruit Tart, and Lemonade (ad libitum)	1/6
14.	Children's Dinners, Melton Mowbray Luncheon Pies, Fruit Tart, and Lemonade (ad libitum)	9d.
15.	Sausage Roll, Custard Tart, Glass of Lemonade	6d.
16.	Bun or Scone, Glass of Milk or Lemonade	3d.

OTHER LUNCHEONS ARRANGED.   PRICES ON APPLICATION.
Light Refreshments can be had at any time of the day at Moderate Charges.

SHELTERED ACCOMMODATION FOR 2,000.
Large Fields open for Cricket, Football, Skipping, etc., Free of Charge.
Amusements charged for :—
DONKEY & PONY RIDING, SWINGS, HELTER-SKELTER, ROUNDABOUTS, etc.
SWEETS, PRESENTS, etc., for RACES, can be had at low prices. Apply to the Proprietor.

Communications to be addressed to :—

The Late ... me ... Folly Farm

Folly Farm was a popular pleasure spot for Londoners on their visits to the countryside. There were all sorts of entertainments laid on. As well as food, there was a fun fair, brake rides and donkey rides.

A large number of local people were employed at Folly Farm to cater for the visitors. The little girl in the centre is Edna Frusher and standing behind her is Lilian Heady who was nanny to Edna and her two brothers.

The men standing in front of the popular swing-boats would have helped drive the herds of pigs that arrived at New Barnet station for dispatch at the Folly Farm abattoir. The pigs were driven from Lancaster Road, along Margaret Road and Park Road and on to the farm. The boy standing on the right in the front row is Charlie Frusher's son Jack.

Folly Farm was developed by New Ideal Homesteads, who built 1,200 houses there. The John Hampden Secondary School was built on part of the site. The school later merged with East Barnet Grammar School to form a comprehensive school.

Hadley Hall in Park Road. In 1929 John Ward founded a religious order here, known as the Confraternity of Christ the King. By 1931 John Ward had founded a school known as St Michael's College. In 1945 the *Daily Mail* reported on a court case which was brought by the parents of Dorothy Bartola, who had become a junior oblate of the confraternity in 1933. Her parents alleged that she had been enticed into joining the community but she pleaded that she had joined willingly.

The mediaeval tithe barn was erected at Hadley Hall early in 1930 for use as a chapel, having been relocated from its original site in Kent. The Abbey Folklore Museum was opened by the Revd J.S.M. Ward in 1934. A New Barnet wheelwright's shop and the smithy from East Barnet village were transferred to the museum in September 1936. Also on display was a sixteenth-century witch's cottage, shown below. After the Second World War the folk park closed and many items were packed away and taken to Cyprus where Ward died. They eventually ended up in Australia in 1956 and the Abbey Museum is now based in Caboolture in Queensland.

The Abbey Museum became part of an arts centre which was founded in 1946 by William F.C. Ohly to provide domestic and professional accommodation for practising artists. Its residents included Lotte Reiniger, the German film animator, as well as painters, sculptors and art teachers. There was also a pottery in the grounds, equipped with an oil-burning kiln. This piece of sculpture, displayed in the Abbey grounds, was designed by Jessie Watkins and was called 'Pisces'. It turned on a plinth and was 8 ft in diameter.

Freddie Pymm and the sculptor admire their handiwork. Jessie Watkins designed several large works of art which were constructed by Freddie Pymm and Michael Gear at their factory in Victoria Road in 1972. This piece was made of steel and was 15 ft high; it was called 'Scorpio Major'.

EAST BARNET

The church of St Mary the Virgin was either built towards the end of the eleventh century or early in the twelfth. At that time the manor of Chipping and East Barnet was owned by the Abbey of St Albans. Following the dissolution of the monastery in 1539 and the subsequent sale of the Manor of Chipping and East Barnet in 1553, the advowson of the church was retained by the crown and to this day rectors continue to be appointed by the monarch. The 'neo-Norman' church tower was added in 1828 and was originally not joined to the church itself. The doorway in the south wall, which was external but has now become an inner doorway, appears to be part of the Norman building. In the surrounding stonework are some rough-cut crosses and other marks which are reputed to be very old. It has been suggested that they record vows made by parishioners or that they are builders' marks but they could well be simple mass dials. These dials were crosses with holes for the insertion of pegs and were used to tell the times of services.

The Norman north wall at St Mary's Church. There are signs of its ancient past in its three slit windows and its doorway with long and short stonework. The doorway under the gallery was reopened in 1911 after having been bricked up for a number of years. The church was damaged in the Second World War but subsequently restored.

Interior of St Mary's. The south wall was pierced in 1868 and the church extended to provide extra accommodation for the boys from the nearby Boys' Farm Home, a number of whom sang in the choir. Memorial tablets to its founder, Colonel Gillum, and to his wife are displayed in the south transept.

St Mary's Church choir, *c.* 1915. One of the choir boys is Bill Taylor, who was for many years a churchwarden. A surpliced choir, with both boys and girls, had been formed by 1889. In 1890 a dispute arose when the churchwarden tried to get the surplices washed at less than the 1*s* 3*d* each which had been paid for 'many years' to Widow Wilshire. He maintained he could get them done at 6*d* each. However, the choir went on strike and won the day and the widow continued her task.

In 1871 the lych gate was erected and the churchyard fenced, at a cost of £130. Some of the cottages belonging to the Boys' Farm Home can be seen on the right. In 1887 C.J. Vinall, probably with the help of Philip Webb, designed the two cottages nearest to the entrance. The two farther back were designed in 1908 by Charles Nicholson to provide accommodation for some of the older boys who had stayed on beyond the age of sixteen to help with running the dairy.

Church Farm farmhouse was built in about 1660. In 1841 Joshua East was farming the surrounding land. Church Farm supplied mules to the army for use in the Crimean war. In 1860 Lt-Col. W.J. Gillum bought the farmhouse and 48 acres and established the Boys' Farm Home, an industrial school for destitute and delinquent children.

Church Hill House was designed by the renowned architect, Philip Webb, and built for his friend Lt-Col. Gillum in the early 1860s. This photograph was taken around the turn of the century by the LCC architect Charles Canning Winmill, a disciple of Webb. The house survived the development of the area in the 1930s but was demolished in the 1940s or '50s, by which time it was known as Trevor Hall after an earlier house.

Church Farm farmhouse was extended and, as the number of boys grew, further buildings were added. Philip Webb designed the schoolhouse and dormitories which were built in 1868 and 1876 respectively. In 1912 a bellcote was added to the schoolhouse by Charles Nicholson in memory of John Hampton Hale, who had been a member of the management committee for thirty-eight years.

THE BOYS' HOME,

CHURCH FARM, EAST BARNET.

CERTIFIED INDUSTRIAL SCHOOL.

UNDER THE INSPECTION OF HER MAJESTY'S SECRETARY OF STATE FOR
THE HOME DEPARTMENT, AND OF THE COUNCIL OF
THE REFORMATORY AND REFUGE UNION.

A SERMON

Will be preached on behalf of the above Institution

ON

SUNDAY MORNING, FEBRUARY 10, 1867,

AT

JESUS CHURCH,

FORTY HILL, ENFIELD,

BY THE

REV. BROOKE LAMBERT,

M.A., B.C.L.,

Incumbent of St. Mark's, Whitechapel.

AFTER WHICH A COLLECTION WILL BE MADE IN AID OF THE
FUNDS OF THE CHARITY.

DIVINE SERVICE WILL COMMENCE AT ELEVEN O'CLOCK.

The Boys' Farm Home received some government support but was largely reliant on voluntary donations. One of its supporters was the Revd Brooke Lambert. As well as individual benefactors the home received money from institutions such as the Worshipful Company of Armourers and Braziers and the Worshipful Company of Salters, and from offertories at church services.

The farmhouse was extended to provide laundries and additional sleeping accommodation. The building survived the transfer of ownership to the local council in 1938, but a fire caused considerable damage and it was demolished in the 1960s.

The swimming pool, *c.* 1910. On Sundays members of the congregation of nearby St Mary's Church would throw coins into the swimming pool for the boys to retrieve. The pool had been built in 1905 but was unheated and open to the elements. The local council took it over in 1938 when the Boys' Farm Home moved elsewhere and in 1973 the pool was enclosed and heated. Since then it has been used for schools and community use.

Trevor Lodge in Church Hill Road was the lodge to Church Hill House, but after Col. Gillum left the area it, together with the main house, took the name of an earlier house and was known as Trevor Hall.

The Boys' Farm Home buildings. In 1938 New Ideal Homesteads bought the Boys' Farm Home and the adjacent land and developed the whole area, except for the central buildings, including the boys' swimming pool, which they passed to the ownership of the local council for community use.

This view of East Barnet shows how the area appeared in the 1930s before development took place. It was taken from a point near Oakleigh Park station and among the trees on the right is Church Hill House.

Church Hill Road. The old route of Church Hill Road used to lead directly to the church gate. It has been straightened and a triangle of grass remains to provide a pleasant spot to view Oak Hill Park and the houses beyond. The friends of St Mary's School have provided a circular seat, and daffodils have been planted by the East Barnet Parish Residents Association.

This row of cottages stood in Church Hill Road opposite the point where Cedar Avenue now joins it. They were bought by the local council in 1929 and the land at the rear became a recreation ground. The local press reported that it was the council's intention to turn the 'historic cottages' into a museum but this project did not materialize and the cottages were demolished.

The back of St Mary's Church Hall, photographed from the garden of 25 Rosslyn Avenue. On the other side of Church Hill Road stand the old cottages which were used as the National School. The rear of the houses built along Church Hill Road in the 1930s are also visible.

This photograph of Church Hill Road shows the front view of the completed houses a little later on but before Rushdene Avenue had been built. During the war a bomb exploded in the park opposite, damaging the roofs of the houses. It was fortunate that this had not occurred the previous evening when a circus had been performing there.

Cottages in Church Hill Road. The building at the end of these cottages was commonly referred to as the Old National School. The cottages were in residential use when they were demolished in 1952. Several buildings were used to house the National School, including the Black Prince Inn (*see* page 80) and a building on Cat Hill. In 1822 a grant of £20 had been paid towards 'the fitting up of a daily school for 56 boys and 56 girls'. A lease of a property was obtained for one year with the option of increasing the period to seven or fourteen years. The building was described as having lathe and plaster front and end walls, a brick back and a tiled roof. It had two classrooms, 22 ft 4 in wide by 14 ft 6 in wide, and was 8 ft 4 in high. It is not clear where this building was or who owned it but it may have connections with the one referred to in 1841 in the estate papers of Edward Beeston Long (held at the Hertfordshire Record Office), in which it is described as 'the schoolhouse now divided into two tenements with gardens' which were sold on 25 October 1841 for £262 10s and let to Solomon Edie at £10 per annum. Piggotts' 1838 Directory shows a National School for boys and girls being run by Mrs McFarlane. The 1841 Census describes Mrs Elizabeth McFarlane as a teacher and by the time of the 1851 Census Ann Treweek, aged 47, seems to have taken over the running of the National School. From at least 1854 a separate building on Cat Hill was being used as an infants' school.

The village pond. A nearby oak was associated with a Joanna Southcott, a 'prophetess' who had vowed in 1814 that she was to be the mother of the promised Messiah. However, she died of dropsy a few months later. In 1932 the local fire brigade was called out to save the ancient oak, which had mysteriously caught fire. The mystery may now have been solved, as Len Baynes, the son of a local builder, confesses in the story of his boyhood to having caused a similar fire with other local lads.

The newly built St Mary's School was opened in 1872. The 1870 Education Act had laid down that school boards were to be established in areas where sufficient places were not available for all children to be educated. The new school in East Barnet was built to provide the extra places that were needed.

Jubilee Terrace, named after Queen Victoria's Jubilee, is the first block of shops on the left side of Church Hill Road. Further along are the clapboarded Sellwood Cottages. A clearance order was issued by the East Barnet Urban District Council in 1935 for 1–6 Sellwood Cottages which were owned by Miss E.D. Allen and 4 and 5 Brook Cottages which were owned by Mr H. Marsh.

East Barnet village, c. 1910. This view shows the Prince of Wales public house with a different façade to that seen today. It also shows the site of the Methodist Church on the corner of Church Hill Road, with the old King's Head public house on the right.

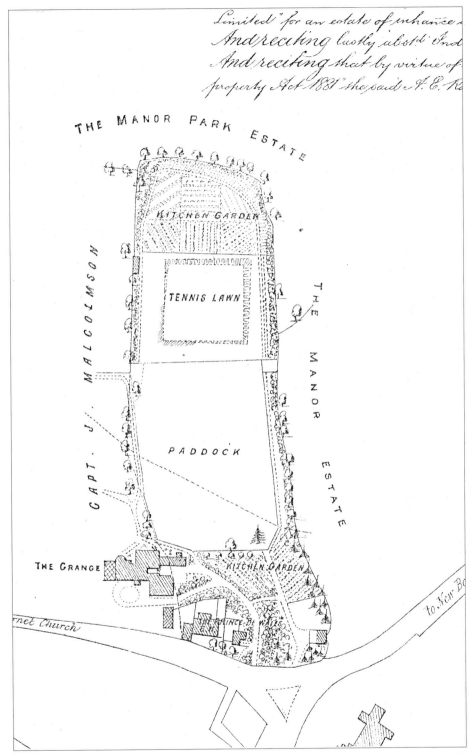

This plan of the Manor Park Estate shows the area where Jackson Road was developed in about 1890 by William Jackson. In 1887 he had acquired land which had previously formed part of the Grange Estate.

The history of the Prince of Wales public house is unclear. It was licensed as a beerhouse called the Black Prince in 1878, but it may date back even further than that; William Jackson was the beer retailer of an unnamed beerhouse in 1866 but in 1872 Thomas Jackson was the licensee of the Black Prince. The brewers were Alfred Pry of Hatfield. The photograph shows the timber framework that was revealed when the building was recently refurbished and the end wall repaired. The timber framework suggests that the building may date back to the eighteenth century. A photograph of 1880 shows the building as a double-fronted house, without the gabled end section. According to the Revd F.B. Cass, the National School became a beerhouse and it is likely that this was the building. This seems to be confirmed by William Stutters who wrote that he could recall a sign on the building which denoted it as the National School. The deeds of the Black Prince from 1805 to 1860 are held at Hertfordshire Record Office.

This view of the village centre was taken from the higher ground near the Cat Inn. On the right the old King's Head public house can be seen, together with the roof and chimneys of the Clockhouse and the bridge over the Pymmes brook. To the left are the backs of the shops in Jubilee Terrace and the houses in Jackson Road.

The East Barnet Brush Works premises behind the cottages in Church Hill Road near St Mary's School, where Winston Court now stands.

The Cat Inn decorated for the coronation in 1953. It had taken its name from the nearby bridge which was mentioned in a will of 1406. The inn was badly damaged by fire in the mid-1950s and after lying derelict for a number of years the site was redeveloped with flats and a shop.

This corner of Church Hill Road and Cat Hill was the site of the tin chapel which served the local Methodists until a church was built on the site. To the right can be seen the end wall of the bakers in Jubilee Terrace. To the left is the old King's Head which was selling an average of seven barrels of beer a week in 1928 when there were attempts to close it down. In the 1930s a newly built pub was set back 3 ft from the pavement to widen the corner and two nearby cottages were demolished to allow the Cannon Brewery to rebuild and extend the pub.

The North Middlesex Automobile Club held a hill-climb up Cat Hill in May 1908. In the top photograph the cars are seen waiting to start, while in the lower picture they are beginning the climb out of the village. The event was judged by Col. Henry F. Bowles JP, and the time-keeper at the finish was Mr J.H. Burley.

The village pump. According to the Barnet Press in 1877 Mr F.S. Parker had complained to the local council that the pump opposite his gateway was disfiguring the village. He offered to pay for the expense of enclosing the ground and planting trees in the enclosure if the Board removed the pump. His offer was accepted and the village war memorial was erected on the site in 1922.

The rear of the Clockhouse. This house was originally called Dudmans and was built by Thomas Dudman during the reign of Henry VIII. In 1821 it was leased by J.H. Fowell of St Albans to Septimus Schollick, a schoolmaster, for twenty-one years. The house was later divided into two, one part being known as Arlington Towers.

The Clockhouse was demolished in 1925. The clock and clocktower were removed and refurbished by Mr Atkins, and later installed over the shops. Here the demolition workers take a break to pose for the camera.

The clock was again repaired and restored by Dan Ruge-Cope in 1986 at the instigation of the East Barnet Parish Residents' Association. In 1996 Mr Ruge-Cope has been repairing the clock face.

These prints show New Place, a house built in 1719 by John Cotton. It was at least the second house built on that estate and it soon reverted to the earlier name of Littlegrove. The gardens were laid out by Lancelot ('Capability') Brown in 1768, for which he received £700. Arthur Young, the famous agriculturist, also advised the owner, Mr Willes, about the garden. Some remains of the mansion's gardens are still visible in the gardens of the houses on Cat Hill and in Ridgeway Avenue. During the First World War Littlegrove was used by the Army. When it was being redeveloped for housing in 1932 the Barnet Press reported 'in the dungeons are a number of gloomy cells each about 6 ft square, the original purpose of which can be readily judged from the sentiments expressed in the writing on the walls. I wonder who the poor fellow was who wrote: "Here I am today, Here I will be tomorrow, Let no man ever say I've not had my share of sorrow".'

Bohun Lodge stood near Bourne Gate, the boundary gate across Cat Hill which led into Enfield Chase. It was referred to as Burnegate in 1270 and Boongate in 1676. In 1926 Bohun Lodge was bought by Charles Baring Young as a place for the preliminary training of prospective candidates for the ministry. In 1937 the house was sold and all the training was concentrated at Oak Hill.

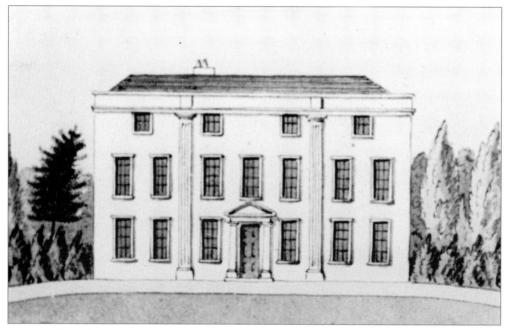

Buskin Hall stood on the edge of Enfield Chase. According to Frederick Cass it may have been the house referred to as being 'lately built, near Sonnesgrove' in 1558. Percival Bosanquet, son of Henry Augustus Bosanquet who lived at Osidge, bought the house in 1870. By then it was called Dacre Lodge but under Mr Bosanquet it reverted to its original name.

Monkfrith House was built as Oak Hill House early in the nineteenth century, although an earlier house on the site is first mentioned in 1565. In the 1930s the later house was demolished and Cedar Rise, Monkfrith Way and Friars Walk were built.

Oak Hill Park. In October 1931 the local council bought 61 acres of land from the Kingham Hill Trust at a cost of £25,000. With a gift of a further 5 acres to the north the park was extended to include the East Barnet recreation ground. The whole area now covers some 74 acres.

Oak Hill House was called Oak Hill Park when it was built towards the end of the eighteenth century, at which time the Monkenfrith estate appears to have been divided into two. It had previously been a deer park, hence the original name. The building is now used as a theological college.

Heddon Court preparatory school was founded in Hampstead in the 1890s by Henry Frampton Stallard, an ex-Indian Army officer. In the 1920s the school moved to East Barnet, into a house then known as Belmont (but previously as Mount Pleasant). The house was enlarged and renamed Heddon Court. From April 1929 until July 1930 John Betjeman was a master at Heddon Court, where he met Vera Spencer-Clarke, to whom he wrote the following poem:

As I was walking through the park
I met Miss Vera Spencer-Clarke;
And since I am the sort of chap
Who's always smart in a mishap,
I said to her, with eyes aflame,
'Now have I met you? What's your name?'
She answered, elegant and proud,
'I do not like the common crowd.'
Not unrebuffed, I further said:
'Now are you yet in wedlock wed?'
What change suffused her noble brow;
She was no simple Vera now,
But like a man she swung her arms,
And masculine became her charms;
With heavy stride she forward strode
And threw my body on the road.
But still I'm praying for the soul
And body too, of Mr Moule.

The cricket field. One of Betjeman's duties was to teach the boys cricket. After an evening out with two colleagues they drove up the stony drive and zig-zagged across the cricket pitch, which had been prepared for a match. The driver of the car, Mr Huxtable, was sacked but Sir John survived the incident and taught here for a further three terms. Sir John's period at the school is commemorated in his poem 'The Cricket Master', extracts of which are included here. He appears in the poem to be looking back somewhat wistfully at his lost youth as well as the changes that had taken place locally. Another of his poems, called 'School Train', was based on his experiences at Heddon Court. At the beginning of term a special Heddon Court carriage was included on the train from London to New Barnet. The carriage was supervised by a master and presumably this was a duty Sir John had performed.

My undergraduate eyes beholding,
As I climbed your slope, Cat Hill:
Emerald chestnut fans unfolding,
Symbols of my hope, Cat Hill,
What cared I for past disaster,
Applicant for cricket master,
Nothing much of cricket knowing,
Conscious but of money owing?
Somehow I would cope, Cat Hill.

Shops and villas have invaded
Your chestnut quiet there, Cat Hill.
Cricket field and pitch degraded,
Nothing did they spare, Cat Hill.
Vera Spencer-Clarke is married
And the rest are dead and buried:
I am thirty summers older,
Richer, wickeder and colder,
Fuller too of care, Cat Hill.

The dining room at Heddon Court. At breakfast some of the staff sat with the headmaster and his wife, while the rest were strategically placed on the boys' tables. The process alternated each week with teachers sitting at High Table one week and on a boys' table the next.

The classroom, c. 1925. Sir John was a somewhat eccentric teacher. He liked to surprise the boys and would on some occasions enter the classroom through the window, and on others teach while lying on the floor.

In 1933 the estate was sold to developers. The names of the roads that were built in the area are linked with the old estate and include Heddon Court Avenue, Heddon Road, Mount Pleasant and Belmont Avenue. The war interrupted the development but it began again after the war and was completed by 1948.

Hill Crest Estate, Cat Hill. This development is advertised as Hadley Woods rather than East Barnet in order to raise its image. However, the houses shown in the advertisement appear to be nos 134 and 136 Cat Hill, which lie on the opposite side of the road to Heddon Court.

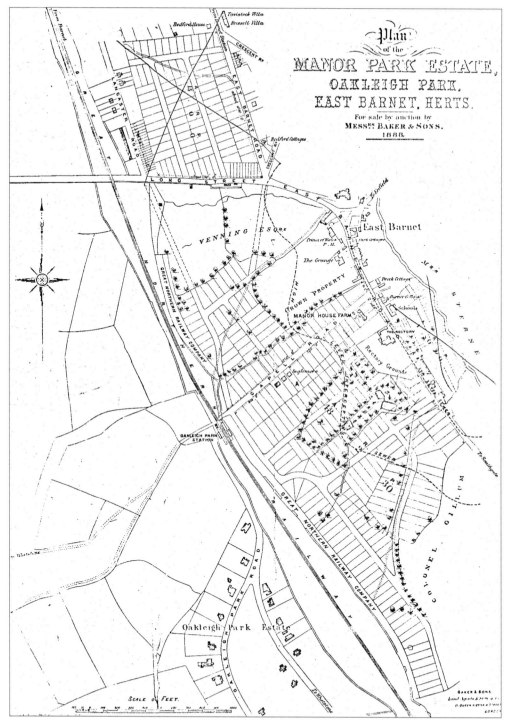

The Manor Park Estate. This plan shows the intended layout of the estate. Although the early development conformed to the plan, development was somewhat protracted and the building that took place in the 1930s was more dense and the road layout was altered. Cedar Avenue joined Church Hill Road further along and Lovelace Road was added.

The four Vinsen sisters lived at Westover, one of the houses Betjeman describes. Here, one of them is standing outside the house, with an unidentified child. Sir John Betjeman, after he had left Heddon Court, used to revisit the area to see old friends. In another of his poems, 'The Outer Suburbs', he describes one visit.

The weary walk from Oakley Park
Through the soft suburban dark
Bedizened with electric lights
Which stream across these Northern Heights.
In blackened blocks against the view
Stands gabled Rosslyn Avenue.
And bright within each kitchenette
The things for morning tea are set.
A stained glass window, red and green,
Shines, hiding what should not be seen,
While wifie knits through hubbie's gloom
Safe in the Drage-way drawing-room,
Oh how expectant for the bed
All 'Jacobethan' overhead!

Westover, now no. 25, was built in 1906 by Mr James Reuben Upton, who built five other houses in a similar style. To the right of the house the roof of St Mary's Church Hall can be seen. This was built in 1910 on land belonging to the old rectory in Church Hill Road.

This view shows Oakhurst Avenue in the distance and the rear of 25 Rosslyn Avenue. Before the 1930s brought further development, the adjacent land was used as tennis courts.

Houses at the top of Lovelace Avenue and Albermarle Avenue were featured in *Town and Country News* in May 1931 when the Oakleigh Park Estate was being developed. The article said: 'Those who are looking for houses in the northern suburbs would do well to examine the merits of the Oakleigh Park Estate, before they get so widely known that all houses are snapped up.' It was the opening of the Underground line to Cockfosters that made the area so popular for development in the 1930s.

Osidge Lane, a quiet country lane, *c.* 1910.
Nearby Osidge House faces Chase Side and in
1834 it was bought by Augustus Bosanquet,
who wrote in his diary on 13 April 1859:
'A year or two ago, when the land opposite was
to be sold, a speculative builder came, as
I suspected at the time, and was assured by his
tenant afterwards, built 4 houses exactly
opposite in the mere hope that the annoyance
I should feel, would compel me to buy them.
I did not think of it and they have been so heavy
on his hands that he seems to have given way
entirely to habits of intoxication. On the other
side of me a cemetery was proposed. The MP
I knew had to bring forward the bill; I told him
the injury that would be inflicted on the
neighbours but he forwarded the scheme.'

The entrance to the Great Northern Cemetery in Brunswick Park Road. In 1855, when burial grounds in
central London had reached capacity, the Great Northern Cemetery Company bought 150 acres of land
on both sides of Brunswick Park Road. The Great Northern Cemetery was opened in 1861, with its own
railway sidings. The GNR had a special building for coffins at Kings Cross and supplied funeral carriages at
the cost of £1 each, subsequently reduced to 10*s*. This scheme was not successful and the sidings were
closed in 1873. The name of the signal box remains Cemetery Box.

These two prints show a train crash near the Standard Telephone Company factory, photographed from the bank by Oakleigh Road North some time after 1955.

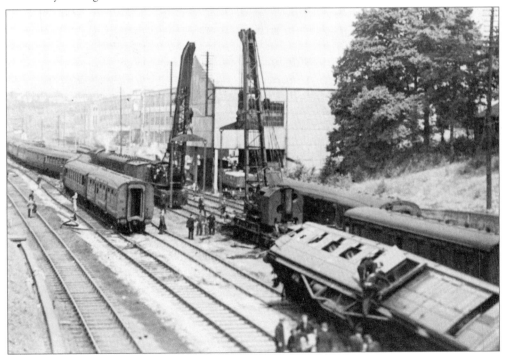

This attractive sketch of of East Barnet village and the dam was drawn by I. Hassell in 1817. The exact location of this view is not known but the writer believes it was probably near the bridge over the Pymmes Brook at the bottom of Cat Hill.

HADLEY

The beacon on the tower of St Mary's Church is lit for significant national occasions such as peace or victory celebrations, coronations, royal marriages or jubilees. This probably shows the beacon lit for the 1971 quincentenary celebrations of the Battle of Barnet.

Hadley Church reflected in the pond in the grounds of Beacon House.

Hadley Hurst, an imposing Queen Anne house, is shown before the addition of the west wing in the 1920s, possibly by Sir Edwin Lutyens. The people in the picture cannot be identified, but are probably members of the family of Wilbraham Taylor Esq., gentleman usher to Queen Victoria. He lived here for most of the second half of the nineteenth century.

Hadley Lodge stands on the north side of the Common near the Gate. Surprisingly for such a grand house, it fronts directly on to the footpath. Destroyed by fire on 19 April 1981, its replacement was not completed until 1996.

Two rather more modest residences are pictured here, but both look very attractive. The upper picture shows the Gate House which stood opposite Hadley Lodge, with the Verger, Mr Heron, in his garden in about 1870. The lower picture shows Gothic Cottage in Dury Road. Early this century this picture appeared in the magazine *Wonderful London* as part of a feature recommending country walks for Londoners on day trips.

At the opposite end of the social scale are these
houses in the designated clearance area between
Taylors Lane and Kitts End Road, photographed
by Eric Daw in 1959. The old tin bath and the
mop and bucket may be misleading, for both
houses are sufficiently up-to-date to have
televisions. The proposed replacement of these
houses by council housing was successfully
fought by local residents, who later formed the
Hadley Residents Association.

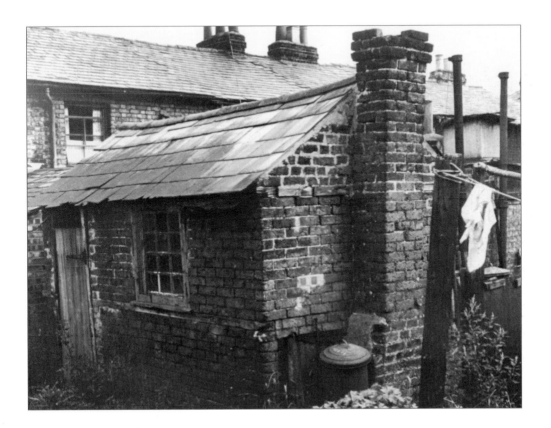

The Infant School on Hadley Green, between Clyde Villas and Ossulston House, pictured in 1933 shortly before its demolition to make way for East View.

Monken Hadley Church of England primary school was founded in 1832 as a National School. It had 58 pupils in 1886, and 90 in 1920, five years before this picture was taken.

The school was rebuilt in 1932 (top) although the lean-to section appears unaltered. There were further additions before 1951, when the lower picture was taken. The adjacent cottages had no connection with the school and have now been demolished to make way for further extensions and a playground.

Latimer's Elm stood adjacent to the Hadley Road Gate, which can be seen in the background. Its name probably derived from the seventeenth-century tenant on whose land it stood. It is recorded as having been struck by lightning and having its top half destroyed in a blizzard. It nevertheless lingered on until it was removed in 1935. Its size can be gauged from the boy in the lower picture and from the fact that it was separately identified on Ordnance Survey maps.

Although the postcard above identifies this tree as the King Edward IV oak, it was more commonly known as Warwick's Oak (and sometimes Elm). It is recorded as having a circumference of 26 ft in 1796 and 27 ft in 1903. It did not long survive the removal of its protective railings in 1941 as part of the war effort. Hadley Lodge and the Gate can be seen in the background.

This picture shows the tree against the background of a cottage known as the Hermitage, which was destroyed in the winter of 1872/3.

This charming bridge over the brook in Hadley Woods has now been replaced by an uglier but sturdier brick creation, which is better able to withstand today's traffic and vandals. Perhaps fortunately, the surrounding trees and bushes have grown so as to make this view unrecognizable today.

The path over the bridge leads you to Gothic Farm, Bakers Hill. Here it is seen in about 1880.

Excavations were carried out at a bank and
ditch in Hadley Wood in 1955. Although the
earthworks were thought to date from the Iron
Age (*c.* 800 BC to AD 43), no positive evidence
was found. Would open sandals and long skirts
be acceptable on an excavation site in today's
health and safety conscious environment?

A wintry view looking north from the corner of Dury Road. On the right is Zitta Cottage, with Hamsher's timber yard beyond.

This picture almost continues from the one above, and shows the scene along the Highstone, with the Windmill public house prominent. Also shown are the premises of Henry Harrisson, who seems not only to have taken over Hamshire's but also to have traded as a builders merchant and undertaker. The post office is shown on the extreme right.

Entitled 'Near Cockfosters', this picture actually shows the lodge gates of what is now the West Lodge Hotel on Ferny Hill, at the junction with Cockfosters Road.

Children fishing in the Brewery Pond in 1934, with Hollybush House in the background and Dr Livingstone's house at the far right.

The post office stood in Crescent West, near Hadley Wood station.

General William Booth (1829–1912), founder of the Salvation Army, lived at Rookstone in the Crescent East during the 1890s. His son, another William, also lived in the Crescent until his death in 1929.

The Gate House and the Gate, seen from the opposite direction to the picture on page 104. It was not a gatehouse in the toll-gate sense but was simply a house near the gate provided for the use of the verger or parish clerk.

Hadley stocks were rebuilt in 1827 to fit two people, but their use was abolished by a law passed in 1837. They remained for nearly another century until they were accidentally destroyed in the bonfire celebrations for the Silver Jubilee of King George V. The pillory and stocks were used as forms of punishment from at least the thirteenth century.

Road accidents are nothing new. This one, early this century, involved a steam traction engine which was either delivering or collecting a wagon load of beer barrels from the Hadley Hotel in Hadley Road. Then, as now, a crowd quickly gathered.

PEOPLE

Geoffrey de Mandeville, Earl of Essex, is said to haunt Oak Hill Park and Hadley Woods every six years. Earl Geoffrey was Lord of the Manor of Enfield and died fighting King Stephen in 1144. His effigy is still to be seen in the Temple Church in the City, and his ghost is next due to make an appearance in 1998. Most Barnet people, if they have heard of Geoffrey de Mandeville at all, will think of him as the red-cloaked knight, the local spectre who haunts Hadley Woods and East Barnet with his headless hound. They may also have heard the legend that Camlet Moat, now quiet and secluded in Trent Park, is the site of Geoffrey's medieval castle. Some people, if they have read certain local history books, might even have come across the theory that Geoffrey de Mandeville was the original Robin Hood.

William Seymour, Marquis of Hertford, 1660.
This original painting by Van Dyke is in the
collection of the Rt Hon. Earl of Clarendon.

Major General Augustin, Provost of Greenhill,
East Barnet. He was born at Geneva and
married Anne, daughter of Chevalier Grand of
Amsterdam. He died on 10 May 1786 aged 63
years, and his large tombstone is in East Barnet
church.

ADMIRAL BYNG.

The Hon. John Byng, Admiral of the Blue. Shot by a marine firing squad on the quarterdeck of HMS *Monarch* on 14 March 1757, Byng was one of the bravest scapegoats ever. His downfall, aided by unscrupulous journalists, is a terrifying example of a government conspiring to 'frame' a commander-in-chief in order to save its own reputation. Augustus Keppel, one of Byng's junior officers, defended Byng and was himself court-martialled on board the *Britannia* in 1779. However, he was found not guilty and honourably acquitted. Admiral Byng built Wrotham House in the Palladian style and the building was completed in 1754. He named it Wrotham after the Kentish village where his family had lived since the time of Henry VII. A transcript of Keppel's trial in 1779 – he was then himself an Admiral of the Blue – can be seen at Barnet Museum.

Admiral Sir George Byng, lst Viscount
Torrington, 1663–1733. Born at Wrotham in
Kent, he entered the Navy at the age of fifteen.
In 1688 he helped to persuade the fleet to rally
to the cause of William of Orange, and was
made a Captain. He was the father of Admiral
John Byng.

George Byng – Lord Torrington.

George Byng, MP. He served as Member of Parliament for Middlesex for fifty-seven years and was the Father of the House of Commons. His father, another George, was a contemporary and colleague of John Wilkes, who was also an MP for Middlesex. George Byng snr inherited Wrotham Park following the execution of Admiral Byng.

General Sir J.H.G. Byng, 1st Viscount Byng, 1862–1932. He was the seventh and youngest son of George Stevens Byng, and the 2nd Lord Strafford. He became Field Marshall Viscount Byng of Vimy, commanding the Third Army in the First World War, and was afterwards Governor General of Canada and Commissioner of the Metropolitan Police.

Col. Frederick Trotter JP, 7th Battalion King's
Royal Rifle Corps, 1838–1900.

Major Frederick Liddell Trotter, King's Royal
Rifle Corps, 1898–1961.

Capt. John Trotter, 1808–1870. According to the Barnet Press in October 1895, 'He gave up a life of worldliness and set his face steadily to do all in his power to redeem the time he had wasted on himself.' In 1844 George Byng of Wrotham sold him some land measuring three roods, twenty-six perches and six yards for £70. The land was part of a close called Four Acre Field, then or previously in the occupation of James Buckle. Capt. Trotter commissioned the famous architect Gilbert Scott to design a church for the site. This was to be Christ Church, Barnet, where David Livingstone and his family worshipped and became friends with the vicar, the Revd William Pennefather. John Trotter, the father of Capt. John Trotter, bought Dyrham Park in 1798. He had made his money by supplying clothing to the army. Almost immediately after he took possession of it, the Elizabethan house was burnt to the ground and rebuilt. According to Nikolaus Pevsner, its design 'looks as if it might be inspired by Inigo Jones's St Paul's, Covent Garden'. Four generations of Trotters held the estate until it was sold in 1938 to the Middlesex and Hertfordshire County Councils as it lay across the border of the two counties.

Revd William Pennefather, born 5 February 1816, died 30 April 1875. In 1852 Revd Pennefather became the vicar of Christ Church. By birth an Irishman, his charismatic appeal soon attracted a large following. Capt. John Trotter and Revd Pennefather probably met in 1847 when Trotter crossed to Ireland to help relieve the famine-stricken people of Connemara. The two men were from very different backgrounds – Mr Pennefather was the son of Baron Pennefather, a Judge in the Court of Exchequer, Dublin, and was brought up in religious surroundings, while Capt. Trotter, to quote the Pennefather Memorial, 'was living only for the world and its pleasures and pursuits when God called him, and he obeyed the call'. Nevertheless, the two men formed a strong alliance and they are buried in adjacent graves at Ridge.

David Livingstone. Having completed his journey across Africa from west to east, and suffering two and a half years of hardship and adventure, he returned to England soon after May 1856 and settled down with his wife and family in Hadley Green. It was here that he wrote an account of his travels during his sixteen years in Africa.

David Livingstone (left) and Wilbraham Taylor. Wilbraham Taylor lived at Hadley Hurst (*see* page 103).

Miss Marjorie Honeybourn MA, FSA, was a history teacher at Queen Elizabeth's Girls' School. Born in Highgate at the turn of the century, she attended Bedford College. She was a member of the Historical Association and also a stalwart member of the London Topographical Society. Responsible for the map of Norman London in Sir Frank Stenton's book *Norman London* published in 1934, she also provided the map in a book entitled *London under Richard II*. Miss Honeybourn lived for a number of years in Highland Road and died in November 1974.

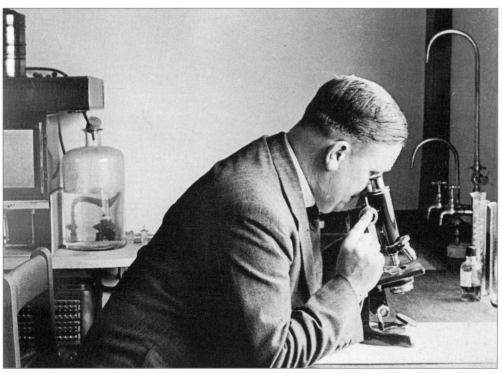

C.M. Barnes, engineer and surveyor, East Barnet Urban District Council. He is pictured in his laboratory at the new sewage disposal works in Brunswick Park Road.

Capt. A. Bellath MSM on his retirement after twelve years as dispenser at Barnet General Hospital.

Sir Thomas Lipton was born in Glasgow in 1850, his Irish parents having travelled to Scotland in a desperate bid to find work. Thomas Lipton started work at the age of ten and within a few years had saved enough money for a steerage ticket to America. He returned to Britain at the age of nineteen and opened his first shop in Glasgow on his twenty-first birthday. The founder of Lipton's Stores, he was nicknamed 'the King's grocer'. He was a sailing companion and adversary of the Prince of Wales, later King Edward VII, but as a commoner he was not allowed to join the Royal Yacht. He lived at Osidge House, which is now a retirement home for nurses.

W.H. ('Bill') Gelder in 1974, aged 62. He was born in Brighouse, Yorkshire, and his family moved to Barnet in 1913. He attended Byng Road School and Queen Elizabeth's Boys' Grammar School. He trained as a teacher at Nottingham University College and for thirty-two years taught at the Cloudesley in Islington, a school for handicapped children, eventually becoming deputy head before retiring. He was a regular contributor to the Barnet Press for fifty-one years, writing reviews of local amateur productions and numerous feature articles on a variety of subjects, including aspects of local history. Many of these were compiled into five books about Barnet and Hadley. He co-wrote and edited *Historic Barnet*, to which eight other Local History Society members contributed. He was made a vice-president of the Society in 1978 and an honorary life member at his eightieth birthday party, held in the museum, where he is a regular steward.

Winifred Attwell, the well-known pianist, with her husband at the Whitsun Carnival at Oakleigh Park in 1951. They lived in Oakleigh Park.

Constance Tipper was born in New Barnet in 1894 and died aged 101. She conducted pioneering research into metal crystals which enabled her to work out why the hulls of liberty ships were splitting during the Second World War. She developed the 'Tipper Test' to determine the vulnerability of steel, and uncovered many of the underlying processes in the crystal grains of the metal.

Lady Enfield and Councillor Earnes at the opening of the 'Help Russia' campaign in a field off Wood Street in 1916. Mrs Poole is second from the left.

H.W. Poole was clerk and solicitor to the Barnet Local Board and Barnet Urban District Council.

Viscount Hampden, the Lord Lieutenant of Hertfordshire, at the official opening of Longmore Avenue (previously Long Street), New Barnet, in May 1931.

Wood Street, *c.* 1880s. The gentleman is seated in an Otto Dicycle of 1877. This design, however, proved to be very impracticable.

St James's United Football Club, 1919.

Lester Finch (in foreground, third from left) after Barnet FC won the FA Amateur Cup on 20 April 1946.

Barnet Football Club, 1951/2. Back row, left to right: D. Platts, D. Lipington, D. Hawkins, F.W. Stevens, M. Whillock, A.S. Blackburn. Front row: D.G. Haskow, R.B. Livermore, J.C. Gerrans (captain), G. Sullivan, J.Garrett.

These two photographs were taken at Barnet Football Club's families Christmas party, *c.* 1946. The party was held at what is now the Conservative Club, next to the Red Lion. Father Christmas was Freddie Pymm, and his two daughters are standing in front of him (in Fair Isle sweaters). The younger of the girls is Gillian Gear, Hon. Secretary of the Barnet & District Local History Society. Ivy Pymm is in the front right corner in the upper photograph.

Five hundred years after the Battle of Barnet, Hadley Women's Institute (Herts.) completed a facsimile of the banner of the victorious Edward IV, which can now be seen in Barnet Museum. This photograph was taken in 1971.

Putting up the new whalebones in Wood Street in June 1939. The jawbones were taken from a 190 ft Blue Whale and weighed 25 cwt. They were ordered by Miss Cowing, then owner of Barnet Press, and were taken from a whale captured in the South Seas. Transhipped to Norway, they arrived at Barnet via Hull.

Barnet fire brigade, *c.* 1918. The old station was in the High Street, near the Monken Holt pub.

East Barnet Valley UDC fire brigade, *c.* 1925

Barnet fire brigade, *c.* 1900. This 'team' photograph includes A.J. Hetherington (*see* below).

The funeral of (Alfred) James Hetherington in 1921. He lived at The Cottage at Friern Barnet sewage works, and was manager of the sewage works from 1890, when it was built, until his death.

Staff of the Barnet Press during a Wayzegoose (printers' outing), between 1910 and 1914. Founded by a member of the Cowing family, Barnet Press was 137 years old in June 1996.

The New Barnet Crusaders Easter camp at Bayfordbury in 1933. Seated, fourth from the left, is F.J. Parsley, who lived at Kheda, Park Road, New Barnet.

Barnet town band, *c.* 1900.

Barnet Town Prize Band, 1907.

James Ripley, ostler at the Red Lion and post office, Barnet, in 1781. In the days when hostelries had exclusively Whig or Tory patrons, the Red Lion was the Tory headquarters while The Green Man, which stands at the other end of the town, was the rendezvous for the Whigs. Pepys' diary entry for 11 August 1667 records that he drank and ate the best cheese cakes he had ever had at the Red Lion, which stood where Fritch's shop is now. Barnet Museum has a collection of James Ripley's letters. To the Hon. Col. Blaithwate and the rest of the Royal Regiment of Horse Guards Blue he wrote: 'and I shall always esteem it an honour to rub down your horses' heels, so long as I am able to stoop to my foot. I think it is universally allowed that the finished Gentleman is to be met with more frequently in the camp than at court: in you the Gentleman, the Soldier, and the Scholar are happily united. May the Royal Regiment of Horse Guards Blue flourish to the last period of time, to be a terror to our enemies and an ornament to the British arms; and may it always be honoured with Officers of equal merit to command the finest corps of private Gentlemen in the universe.' In April 1775 a 'Friend to Merit' wrote of James Ripley:

> When in your youth you aspired in quest of fame
> And as a sportsman bravely met your game
> By envy led, Critics in swarms contend
> To find out faults they know not how to mend
> Whilst as an eagle soaring in the sky
> You dare their spleen and all their rage defy.

The licensee of the King's Head, East Barnet, with her family, *c.* 1898. Left to right: Station Sergeant Fred Denyer, Lucy Denyer, Frank Denyer, Mrs Lucy Denyer.

Mr Gilmour, postmaster and tollgate-keeper at the Griffin public house, photographed with his children.

This is the Indenture of Thomas Pratt to Frank Denyer:

This Indenture witnesseth that Thomas Pratt of 2 Railway Cottages, Hadley Wood, age 16 years 9 months, of his own free will and accord, and with the consent of his father Edward Pratt of the same address, doth put himself as an outdoor and workshop apprentice to Frank Denyer of 30 East Barnet Road, New Barnet, Herts, Motor Engineers for the term of four years commencing on the 1st December 1922 and ending on the 2 December 1926 to learn the art of an engineer during which time the said Thomas Pratt shall faithfully serve his master, his secrets keep, his lawful commands obey.

1   Shall do no damage to his master, nor see to be done by others but to his favour shall let or give warning to his said master of the same.
2   Shall not wilfully waste the goods of his said master nor lend them to anyone.
3   Shall not do any act whereby his said master may have any loss with his said master's goods or others during the said term.
4   Shall not absent himself from his said master's services during the hours herein mentioned, unlawfully except through accident or illness in which case all wages are to cease. But in all things as a faithful apprentice, shall behave himself towards his said master during the term.
5   That the said Thomas Pratt agrees with the consent of his Father and to work during the months commencing the First of December 1922 and ending on the 2nd December 1926 for 50 working hours per week.
6   The said Frank Denyer will provide all tools necessary for the said Thomas Pratt's use which are to be left in good condition at the expiration of the aforesaid period, viz 4 years.
7   To pay the said Thomas Pratt the first year 2/6d two shillings and sixpence, for the second year 3/6 three shillings and six pence per week, and the third year 5/- five shillings per week, with the fourth year 6/- six shillings per week. The payment to commence on the 8th day of December 1922.
8   And for the true performance of all and every of the said covenants and agreements either of the said parties bind himself unto the other by those present.
9   Time starts at 8 am to 7 pm, dinner time 1 pm to 2 pm. Thursday 8 am to 1 pm.
10   Holidays 1 week each year.

Signed: Frank Denyer, Edward Pratt
Witnesses: Lucy Denyer, Sarah Pratt

Herts. Cottage Laundry horse and cart in Puller Road, Barnet, *c.* 1912.

J. Welch, fruiterer and coal merchant. The firm also operated as undertakers, and in 1929 J. Welch & Sons also became haulage contractors. This photograph was taken at 49 Puller Road, Barnet.

QUEEN ELIZABETH'S GRAMMAR SCHOOL, BARNET. - Form Group, July, 1901.
1.   2.   3.   4.   5.   6.   7.
Row: ? ? Heber, ? S.J.Bloomfield, G.R.Iago, D.L.Drew, L.W.Webb, G.S.Beach,
        1.   2.   3.   4.   5.   6.
Row: J.W.Bonner, E.L.Newton,?A.P.Ford, A.R.Bothwell, C.R.Merrill,?A.M.Tho
        7. Everest,   8. ? Cuffe,   9. ? D.L.Leith.
Row: 1.   2.   3.   4.   5.   6.   7.
        Cook, Mr. C.G.Kiddell, Weston, A.D.Aylward, Rowley, F.H.Pyle, W.J.Tay
        8. A.V. Cooper. 9. G.H. Bumby. 10. A.S.Martin Smith.

A class photograph from Queen Elizabeth's Grammar School, July 1901.

The teaching staff at Queen Elizabeth's Grammar School, November 1922. Back row, left to right: D.P. Coulton, J.H. Stephens, F.A. Collier, H.I. Judson. Seated: P.W. Scott, Miss Buxton, H.W. Normanton, O.J. Gardner, G.W. Harrison, W. Lattimer (headmaster) J.L. Howson, P. Knowles, J.A. Strugnell, R.G. Ruscoe.

The official opening by Prince George of Kent of the new building at Queen Elizabeth's Boys' Grammar School in 1932. Left to right: Sir Joseph Priestley, Cllr Harold Fenn, Prince George. In the background can be seen the original charter granted by Queen Elizabeth I to the Earl of Leicester for the establishment of a 'free' school in Barnet. (Free schools were free from religious control.)

On 17 November 1957 Queen Elizabeth II visited Queen Elizabeth's Girls' Grammar School. This was said to be the first occasion on which royalty had visited a state school. The Queen is seen here with Miss Freda Balaam, the headmistress, Alderman Harold Fern and others.

Commemoration of the 350th anniversary of the foundation of Queen Elizabeth's Grammar School in 1923. The photograph shows scholars entering St John the Baptist's Church for the service.

'Old Boys' from Queen Elizabeth's Grammar School, photographed in 1919. From left to right: 'Curley' Mays (caretaker at the school), J. Kennedy, A. Smitheram, Sgt Hale. Seated in front is Lt W.W. Bissell. Kennedy and Smitheran were both pupils at the school.

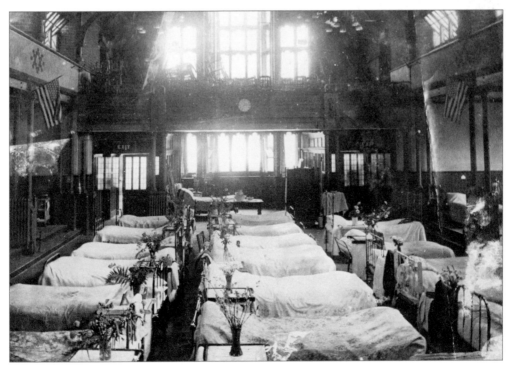

Ewen Hall, Barnet, was used as a Voluntary Aid Detachment hospital in 1918 and 1919. There were seventy beds available.

Queen Elizabeth's Grammar School Cricket XI, July 1880. The captain was S.S. Smith and the scorer H.A. Hildebrand. The photograph was taken outside Tudor Hall, which was originally the free Grammar School of Queen Elizabeth I, but is now part of the Barnet College complex.

Elizabeth Allen Infants' School (also known as the National School), Barnet, 1914. Elizabeth Allen died in about 1727, nearly a century before her school was built. A widow who owned land in her own right, she bequeathed this area for the building of a free school in Barnet, provided that her brother, Josiah Spranger, should die without issue. Josiah obligingly did so.

Hansom cabs waiting outside Barnet station, *c.* 1900.

A day out in 1910. This horse-drawn charabanc is leaving the Monkenholt Arms, formerly The Bell and now the Old Monkenholt. The landlord at this time was Bert Barber.

Two photographs of Barnet's postmen and telegraph boys, 15 May 1909.

Telegraph boys. They were made redundant
years ago and the telegraph itself died with the
advent of telemessages.

In 1890 Barnet post office stood on the east side of the High Street.

ACKNOWLEDGEMENTS

Members of the Executive Committee of the Barnet & District Local History Society have worked together on compiling the various sections and copying the photographs. The first three sections were compiled by Gillian Gear, the fourth by Brian Green and the last by Pat Alison. We are grateful to others, mainly members of the society, who have loaned photographs for use in the book and have given us the benefit of their advice. They include Jeanine Barnes, Joy Bennetts, J. Brandon-Jones, Julian Byng, Jennie Lee Cobban, Jane Downey, Bill Gelder, J. Heather, Dr John Kent, K.P. Kingdon, J. Heady, Edith Spencer, Doreen Willcocks. The photographs were copied by Alan Jaques. The reconstructed map was produced by our chairman, Peter Willcocks. We would like to thank John Murray (Publishers) Ltd for kind permission to print extracts from the poems of Sir John Betjeman.

We hope that readers enjoy this new collection of photographs. We have endeavoured to check and recheck our facts but inevitably there may be errors. If so, we apologize. Any corrections or further information about any of the photographs would be gratefully received by the Society and should be addressed to the Museum.

BIBLIOGRAPHY

Barnet & District Local History Society, *60 Years of Local History, 1927–1987*

Betjeman, John, *Continual Dew* (Murray, 1977)

Betjeman, John, *John Betjeman's Collected Poems* (Murray, 1980)

Chambers Encyclopaedia

Chipping Barnet Parish Church History & Guide (1965)

Daw, Eric, *Barnet High Street in the Early 20th Century*

Gear, G. & Goodwin, D., *East Barnet Village* (Barnet & District Local History Society, 1980)

Gelder, W.H., *Georgian Hadley* (Barnet Press Group, 1974)

Gelder, W.H. (ed), *Historic Barnet* (Muir's Bookshop, 1984)

Hillier, Bevis, *Young Betjeman* (Murray, 1988)

Joliffe, Graham & Jones, Arthur, *Hertfordshire Inns & Public Houses* (Hertfordshire Publications, 1995)

Kelly's Directories

Ripley, James, *Letters*

Taylor, P. & Corden, J., *Barnet, Edgware, Hadley & Totteridge* (Phillimore, 1994)

Tripp, Cecil, *A History of Queen Elizabeth's Grammar School* (Cambridge, 1955)

Turner, Roger, *Capability Brown* (Weidenfeld & Nicolson, 1985)

Warren, Brian, *Notes on the History of Christ Church*

Widdicombe, S.H., *A Chat about Barnet and its History* (The Barnet Press, 1912)

Willcocks, Doreen *Barnet in its Street Names* (Barnet & District Local History Society, 1995)

Barnet & District Local History Society Bulletins

INDEX